In Praise of
SILENCE

PAUL PALMAROZZA

Rev. date: 12/01/2014

To order additional copies of this book, contact:
Xlibris
0-800-056-3182
www.xlibrispublishing.co.uk
Orders@ Xlibrispublishing.co.uk

In Praise of Silence

A collection of ancient and modern
Wisdom regarding the subtle subject
of Silence, drawn from a wide range
of cultures, spiritual traditions and
inspired individuals.

COMPILED & EDITED BY:

Paul Palmarozza

PUBLISHED BY:

Paul Palmarozza

DEDICATION

This work is dedicated to my uncle Henry who first introduced me to a Silent Retreat, to my wife Judica who is a living example of the value of silence and stillness in life and to the School of Economic Science, who over the last 40+ years have provided this person and many others with the finest spiritual education along with the opportunity to practice silence and stillness in loving and supportive Good Company.

May the knowledge provided by the wise people quoted here inspire and guide you.

May All Be Happy

Contents

Introduction

The real motivation for undertaking this project, to praise and extol the virtues of silence, has come from my own personal experience of the many benefits it brings.

The real power of silence was first acknowledged by me when I was 18 years old. My uncle, who had acted as my godfather when I was formally confirmed in the Catholic religion, asked me if I would accompany him on a weekend silent retreat to be held at a local Jesuit monastery. It was the first time he had attended such an event and was looking for company. He probably also thought that it would do me some good. How right he was.

The retreat was attended by about 100 men who, except for a meeting on Saturday evening when questions could be asked, maintained total silence for the weekend. I was greatly surprised about how easily we were able to communicate without words.

What I also discovered as the weekend progressed was how my mind gradually became quieter and at the same time more clear. I decided that the best use of my time would be to undertake some self- examination. This took the form of a reflection on my life, considering what had transpired so far, the main lessons learned and what might be the best direction for the future.

What happened was that the silence and the good company created the ideal conditions for such a reflective activity. I wrote down the findings in the form of notes to which I might refer in the future, as a reminder. It was a beautiful experience in that the thoughts and then the written words just seemed to flow quite naturally, without any effort. There was a clarity which enabled me to see and acknowledge both the good and not so good behaviours of my past.

It was the honesty and the natural humility in which the observations were made that surprised; there were no claims or criticisms. As a result of that initial experience I became a convert to the power of silence and for the next 12 years continued to accompany my uncle on our yearly silent retreat.

When I moved from the US to Brussels just before my 30th birthday I was fortunate enough to find the School of Practical Philosophy, which is associated with the School of Economic Science, a London- based educational charity, founded in 1937. This school provides a marvellous inclusive programme of practical, cultural and spiritual material drawn from philosophies, religions and spiritual traditions of the East & the West.

Part of the study programme are weekend and week-long retreats. While the regular retreats are not run in silence, significant opportunities are offered for quiet reflection and, most importantly meditation, the exercise par excellence for helping to bring one to real silence and stillness.

Attendance at this school as both a student and later as a tutor has continued for more than 40 years. In recent years yearly silent retreats have been organised which I have attended regularly. It is one of the highlights of my year.

In gathering material for this offering I became aware of two main points: the strong current aversion in our society to silence and stillness, and also the extensive coverage of the subject over time by many of the great sages and spiritual guides as well as by astute observers of human nature.

I attended a lecture some 30 years ago by a prominent Ayurvedic medical practitioner, who said the next big medical problem in highly industrialised countries would be mental illness. He said that continual physical and mental activity in our lives without appropriate rest would cause great stress and tension within and which if continued unabated, would result in debilitating mental health problems. He offered as a suggested remedy that we introduce a greater element of silence and stillness into our lives, with meditation being one of the best ways to do this.

Here are two items I discovered through a quick scan on the web about the current situation in the UK regarding mental health problems: *(The Centre for Economic Performance's Mental Health Policy Group)*

Among people under 65, nearly half of all ill health is mental illness.

In other words, nearly as much ill health is mental illness as all physical illnesses combined.

Mental illness is generally more debilitating than most chronic physical conditions.

On average, a person with depression is at least 50% more disabled than someone with angina, arthritis, asthma or diabetes. Mental pain is as real as physical pain and is often more severe.

This work is essentially a compilation of the wise words of others, my role being to simply integrate them into a cohesive whole so that readers can access guidance on how silence can benefit our lives. May their words encourage readers to quietly reflect on their meaning and be brought to that same silence and stillness.

What is silence?

Silence is always present. It is the source, the substance, from which all sounds arise; sounds in the form of thoughts, and verbal sounds in the form of speech. Sounds are vibrations i.e. movements. When there is silence there is stillness. Both silence and stillness are characterised by no movement.

In silence there are no thoughts, just being.
In total silence the mind comes upon the eternal.
- *Krishnamurti*

In silence there is no other: the sense of separateness disappears. We are 'alone'-all one. Silence is rest. It preserves us from exhaustion which is the result of excessive activity, a common state in this current age. Human beings, in fact all beings, need to have a balance of movement and sound with stillness and silence. Through silence we connect with the unseen, the unmanifest.

To experience deep silence is to come into contact with the beginnings of things. Silence brings us in touch with our inner self; it is the source of real joy. It awakens us to the present moment from which a creative impulse and inner knowledge can arise.

The equivalent of external noise is the inner noise of thinking.
The equivalent of external silence is inner stillness.
- *Eckhart Tolle*

Silence is not created. It always exists in its fullness. To access silence we need to stop the noise which covers it, as the clouds cover the sun. In this move from noise and movement to silence and stillness, thoughts are lessened and a spaciousness is created where there is no sound or movement. This space widens and expands until there is only one silent, still substance embracing the entire being. In that deep silence there is real peace and contentment.

The levels of silence are many but for each of us, whoever and whenever we are, silence brings peace to our minds and purpose to our lives. Reaching our spiritual roots or original identity is the aim of silence. Through silence we can stop the over-talking, over- thinking, over-doing and over-the-top emotions.

This works because silence frees the intellect to do 3 things: to observe, to discern and to choose.
- *Anthony Strano*

It is said in various spiritual traditions that creation is brought into existence through sound, e.g. '**In the beginning was the Word.**' Where there is sound there is creation. While sound is the basis for creation it is on the surface. Silence, its source, is at the core. It is like a blank page before the first word is written. Silence gives us access to a space which is beyond creation, a dimension which is beyond life and death.

Let silence take you to the core of life..
- *Rumi*

One who keeps silence will be rewarded with salvation.
- *Muhammad*

It is clear to those who have practiced silence that it is important to bring the outer being to stillness if we are going to be able to quiet the inner self. This does not mean that we are not active. It simply means that the unnecessary distractions are eliminated so that one's full attention can be brought to bear on the task at hand.

Words and questions come from the mind and hold you there. To go beyond the mind you must be silent and quiet. Peace & silence, silence & peace- that is the way beyond.
- *Nisargadatta*

Some additional quotes:

Silence heals; silence soothes; silence comforts; silence purifies; silence revitalizes us.
- *Dada J.P. Vaswani*

Silence is the mother of truth.
- *Benjamin Disraeli*

Silence
It has a sound, a fullness.
It's heavy with sigh of tree, and space between breaths.
It's ripe with pause between birdsong and crash of surf.
- *Angela Long*

I have always loved the desert. One sits down on a desert sand dune, sees nothing, hears nothing. Yet through the silence something throbs, and gleams.
- *Antoine de Saint-Exupéry*

We're not very much into silence in Judaism but I do spend a lot of time listening to God in silence.
- *Rabbi Jonathan Sachs*

Silence is the invisible door to God.
Silence is the inner door to become one with God."
- *Swami Dhyan Giten*

Connecting with the Silence Within.

Silence

- has a calming effect on body, mind and heart
- gives rest to the body, stillness to the mind and openness to the heart
- produces fine energy, clarity of mind and a loving, generous heart.

Resting in silence creates a substance and an inner space which enables us to operate more effectively and more importantly, helps us to unfold our higher nature. In true silence, the intellect, the moving mind and the emotions are still. In this stillness all our ideas and emotions about the creation are eliminated and we are left with a clear memory of our true nature, which is not those many ideas we have gathered over time.

When desire, doubt, or fear is present there are thoughts, sounds in the mind, and emotional movements. The absence of sounds in the physical and subtle realms has a calming effect, offering the gift of tranquillity. Verbal and mental silence opens up our awareness of our true self, so that we may enter a space which is filled with light, knowledge, and consciousness.

Silence is the true friend that never betrays.
- *Confucius*

The person who dares to be silent can come to experience that which is unhindered by experience, craving, or prejudice. When they are absent, there is nothing but love and reason, which are silent and still. The truth of this can only be found by the practice itself, and even then it cannot be expressed in words..
- *John Lane*

Continual imposed verbal silence will not in itself lead to true peace. What is required is that we still the body, mind, and emotions, so that the true underlying silence can be accessed. From this still centre external sounds and activities can be observed, witnessed, and responded to without comment. The result is a state of peace and contentment.

Without silence, there cannot be any real appreciation in life, which is as delicate in its inner fabric as a closed rosebud.
- *Deepak Chopra*

To still the body, mind, and heart requires quiet contemplation, a refining and quieting of the senses and the mind, so that we are able to experience fully the soundless silence.

The wise should always be one with that silence where words together with the mind turn back without reaching it, but which is attainable by the Yogins. Who can describe That which is beyond words? Or if the essence of the phenomenal world were to be described, even that is beyond words. This, to give an alternative definition, may be termed silence, which is known by the sages to be inseparable from Atman.
- Aparokshanubhuti, *Sri Shankaracharya*

The practice of mental silence refreshes our mind and quickens our inner faculties. It is why many philosophic and spiritual traditions recommend a pause, a moments silence, before any task. It is usually recommended that there also be a pause at the end of any action which sets the best basis for the beginning of the next task.
- Swami Paramananda

A vow of silence is usually a religious vow, commonly taken in a monastic context, to maintain silence. Known as Mauna in Hinduism, Jainism, and Buddhism, the practice is also integral to many Christian traditions. Pythagoras, the pre-Socratic Greek philosopher, imposed a strict rule of silence on his disciples. Some religious traditions claim that silence should be kept in order to better speak with God. The claim is that the unguarded tongue dissipates the soul, rendering the mind almost, if not quite, incapable of prayer. The mere abstaining from speech, without this purpose, would be the "idle silence" which St Ambrose so strongly condemns. The disciplined practice of silence involves much self-denial and restraint and is therefore a more wholesome practice, and as such is more useful.

Some additional quotes:

In the silence of the heart God speaks. If you face God in prayer and silence, God will speak to you. Then you will know that you are nothing. It is only when you realize your nothingness, your emptiness, that God can fill you with Himself. Souls of prayer are souls of great silence.
- *Mother Teresa*

Speech is silver, Silence is golden;
Or as I might rather express it:
Speech is of Time, Silence is of Eternity.
Silence is a source of Great Strength.
-*Lao Tzu*

Spiritual study in solitude combined with regular entering into silence, properly conducted, will develop that Truth, that Consciousness, whereby the sins, sorrows, thoughts of body and bodily fears will fall off as a scab when the wound is healed.
- *Swami Rama Tirtha*

When the mind is still and quiet the totality, the completeness of life is experienced and then there is true freedom, peace and bliss.
- *Eckhart Tolle*

Yoga is the settling of the mind into silence. When the mind has settled, we are established in our essential nature, which is unbounded Consciousness. Our essential nature is usually overshadowed by the activity of the mind.
- Patanjali

Make peace with silence, and remind yourself that it is in this space that you'll come to remember your spirit. When you're able to transcend an aversion to silence, you'll also transcend many other miseries. And it is in this silence that the remembrance of God will be activated.
- Wayne W. Dyer

The water in a vessel is sparkling; the water in the sea is dark. The small truth has words which are clear; the great truth has great silence.
- Rabindranath Tagore

It is only in alert silence that truth can be.
- Krishnamurti

Your mind has a flood of questions.
There is but one teacher
Who can answer them.
Who is that teacher?
Your silence-loving heart.
- Sri Chinmoy

When you are in contact with your inner silence, you just know what you should do - you do not have to think about it, and you do not need to compare the pros and cons - you just know.
- Swami Dhyan Giten

Space and silence are two aspects of the same thing. The same no-thing. They are the externalization of inner space and inner silence, which is stillness: the infinitely creative womb of all existence.
- Eckhart Tolle

There is a silence where hath been no sound,
There is a silence where no sound may be,
In the cold grave—under the deep, deep sea,
Or in wide desert where no life is found,
Which hath been mute, and still must sleep profound;
No voice is hush'd—no life treads silently,
But clouds and cloudy shadows wander free,
That never spoke, over the idle ground:
But in green ruins, in the desolate walls
Of antique palaces, where Man hath been,
Though the dun fox or wild hyaena calls,
And owls, that flit continually between,
Shriek to the echo, and the low winds moan—
There the true Silence is, self-conscious and alone.
- *Thomas Hood*

Do you want to change the world? Then change yourself first.
Do you want to change yourself? Then remain completely silent inside the silence-sea.
- *Sri Chinmoy*

Move outside the tangle of fear-thinking. Live in silence.
- *Rumi*

Let us be silent, that we may hear the whispers of the gods.
- *Ralph Waldo Emerson*

Silence is the great teacher, and to learn its lessons you must pay attention to it. There is no substitute for the creative inspiration, knowledge, and stability that come from knowing how to contact your core of inner silence.
- *Deepak Chopra*

Silence is as deep as eternity, speech as shallow as time.
- *Thomas Carlyle*

Meditation

When we are able to become silent within and deeply rest in our being, the experience is one of peace and unity. The finest means for attaining this peace and unity is meditation.

The journey of meditation is a journey to depth, which is a depth both of understanding and of being.
- Fr John Main

A very important resource for humanity today is meditation. Many people try to practise meditation to enable them to better cope with the overactive, stressful world. Meditation speaks of the state of being rather than a practice. It is the perfect antidote to a deluded world captivated by materialism.

Meditation is meant for the chief aim of human life. The coarse world of our senses and the pleasures it gives, do not fulfil this aim, so we need something besides. The reason for the discontent is that the world of pleasure is small and temporary compared with the Divine Self.
- Sri Shantananda Saraswati

While there are many different forms of meditation, the essence of the discipline is to focus our attention on one point, be it the light of a candle or the sound of a mantra. Thoughts will inevitably come to mind which can become a distraction, and the work is to let these thoughts pass and maintain one-pointed attention.

In the case of mantra-based meditation, continual concentration on the sound as it refines, changes from the individual sounding the mantra to a state where one is listening to the mantra and following it. As the process becomes finer the vibrations of the mantra become longer and deeper, filling the entire being. Following to its conclusion, the mantra brings the person to total silence and stillness, a state of total unity. At this point there is no more individual meditating: there is simply One, Eternal Presence.

Meditation is silence, energising and fulfilling. Silence is the eloquent expression of the inexpressible.
- Sri Chinmoy

In silence, relating to God becomes more than thought, dialogue or contractual bargaining.
- Fr Laurence Freeman

The truly great man dwells on what is real and not on what is on the surface.
- Lao Tzu

The simplicity of meditation makes it suitable for people of all ages, including young children; for people of all religious backgrounds; and for those in all walks of life. As recently as 30 years ago, the practice of meditation was generally considered a spiritual exercise mainly for monks and hermits.

Its use now by many people all over the world is one of the more positive aspects of our free, open societies with our extensive facilities for global communications. We have access to a great wealth of spiritual knowledge from all the world's traditions. The problem for us is to find the right way, one suited to our background and individual disposition and then most importantly to fully adhere to the principles and practices of that way. This commitment and discipline are most difficult to sustain, given the many distractions in today's society.

Meditation is offered to children so that they might discover how to be inwardly free and deeply at ease within themselves. The practice does not involve any religious content and allows pupils to discover the utter simplicity of being; abandoning for a while the busy activity of the mind.
- *Laura Hyde, Former Headmistress*

Everything in the world begins and ends with silence. Stillness is at the heart of education.
- *David Boddy, Former Headmaster*

Here are the observations of a number of people who practise meditation. They appear in **Reflections,** a book published by The School of Meditation.

Meditation has given me insight into who I really am. It has changed my life. Not in any dramatic way, but through a very subtle shift in awareness, which informs everything that I do in my life now.
- *Company Director*

When you connect with the stillness, and emotions and thoughts die down, there is a nothingness which is not empty, but full, alive with potential and love.
- *Secretary*

Meditation is the single most useful thing I have ever come across. Over time its practice has helped me to see the movements of my mind more clearly, free from my ideas about them. In my experience it eliminates fear and produces freedom to act more naturally.
- *Design Engineer*

Meditation brings us to the bedrock of our being, a place of lightness, confidence and peace. From this place the setbacks and demands of life become transformed into opportunities to serve each other and the world.
- *Drama Therapist*

Meditation within the Christian tradition has been re-invigorated in recent years due in large part to the efforts of Fr John Main and the current leader of the World Community for Christian Meditation, Fr Laurence Freeman.

Here are some excerpts from **The Heart of Creation** by *Fr John Main*.

The early monastic Fathers soon discovered that one of the hurdles that every man and woman of prayer must surmount is what they described as acedia, which embraces the notions of boredom, dryness, lack of satisfaction, a feeling of hopelessness, of not making any progress.

This sense of boredom, which is very prevalent in our current society, brings about a sense of restlessness and distraction-just the opposite of what is offered through the practice of quiet contemplation. The early Fathers knew that boredom comes from 'desire', the desire to have, to know, to enjoy. They also knew through experience that quiet prayer reduced desire by bringing one closer to the Source of all, which provided full peace and contentment, leaving no place for desire.

This state where one has given up seeking satisfaction in the creation was called apatheia. This state is one of detachment, where we are not possessed by our possessions, where we are without desire. Meditating, we let go of the desire to control, possess, dominate. In order to do this we must learn a most demanding discipline, that is the way of silence and stillness.

Fr John Main also offered some useful guidance about mantra meditation.

A day will come when the mantra ceases to sound and we become lost in the eternal silence of God. The rule when this happens is not to possess this silence or to use it for one's own satisfaction.

Gradually the silences become longer and we are simply absorbed in the mystery of God. The important thing is to have the courage and generosity to return to the mantra as soon as we become self-conscious of the silence.

Every great spiritual tradition has known that the human spirit begins to aware of its own source only in profound stillness. In the Hindu tradition the Upanishads speak of the spirit of the One who created the universe as dwelling in our heart. The same Spirit is described as the One who in silence is loving to all.

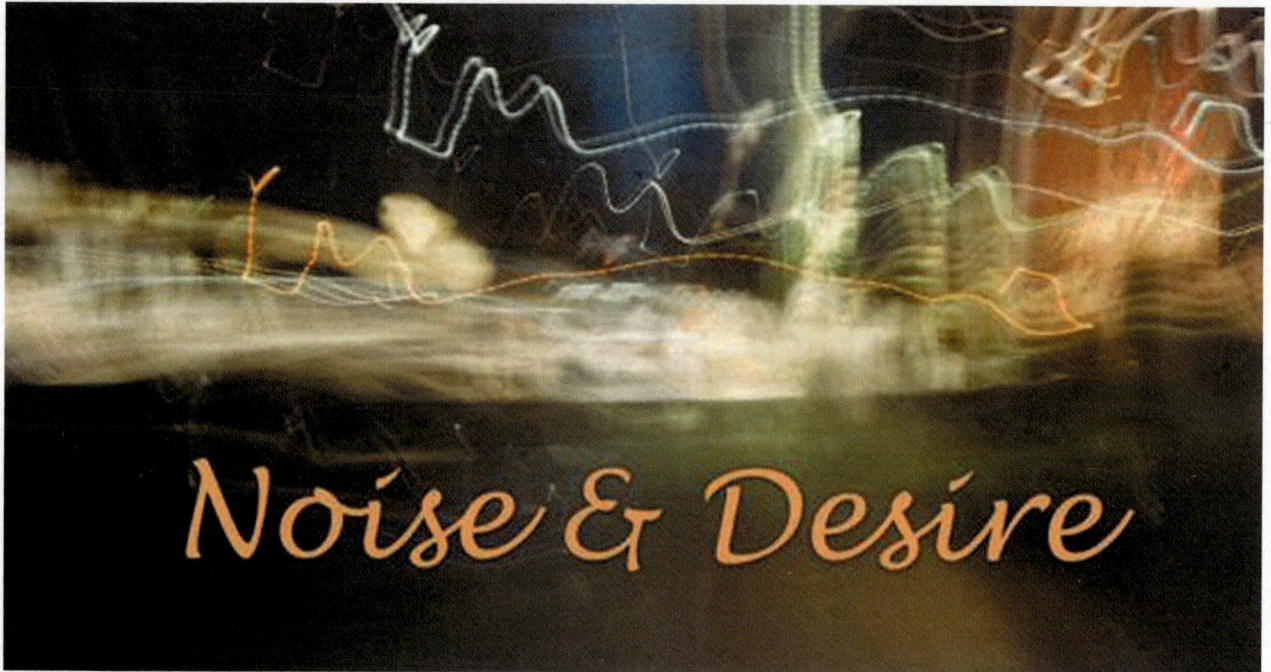

Noise & Desire

The Enemies of Silence – Noise and Desire

Today silence and stillness are not given an honoured and essential place in our lives. They have at various times in the history of our culture been greatly valued, but today our age is hostile to them. We are addicted to noise and movement and cannot accept their absence. We belong to a restless culture with life that is firmly attached to a steady stream of activities, sensory experiences and material possessions. We are uncomfortable in silence and stillness.

Noise has become an increasingly dominant factor in our society. Since the time of the industrial revolution the increase in noise and incessant activity has expanded like the ripples of water when a stone is thrown into a pond. Increasingly a premium has been set on speed, and in this context it is a major sin to waste time. Every moment counts, and so every moment needs to be filled with activity aimed at getting results.

Look how the cult of speed has been served by the major inventions of the last hundred or so years, all designed to allow us to do more in our allotted time:

- Transportation - cars, trains, planes, rockets;
- Communications - telegraph/phones/mobiles/internet;
- Food Preparation - gas cookers/electric ovens/microwaves.

Faster and faster; which leaves little space for silence or stillness.

Without silence there is lack of lasting satisfaction, which we mistakenly try to find through more activities, entertainment and possessions, thus further compounding the problem.

Silence and solitude have never been more important. They preserve us from the world of continual stimulation which results in exhaustion, fanaticism and restlessness. They liberate us from agitation and preserve us from excess.
- John Lane

One of the great 'miss-takes' of our age is to assume that happiness will come from doing, knowing, and enjoying. All these involve an activity of the body, mind, and/ or emotions. True happiness actually arises in silence when there are no distractions and nothing to engage the mind in activity allowing the mind to fall still. In fact, that is when the quality of our doing, knowing, and enjoying is at its finest level.

Here is a view from **Meditations On a Monk Who Dwells in Daily Life** *by Thomas Moore:*

Silence is not an absence of sound. That would be to imagine it negatively. Silence is the toning down of inner and outer static, noise that occupies the ears but also the attention. Silence allows many sounds to reach awareness that otherwise would go unheard; the sounds of birds, water, wind, trees, frogs, insects and chipmunks, as well as conscience, daydreams, intuitions, inhibitions and wishes. One cultivates silence not by forcing the ears not to hear, but by turning up the volume on the music of the world and the soul.

Silence for many is strange and unattractive. Note how many expressions there are to describe our uncertainty about silence: Uncomfortable silence, Awkward silence,

Embarrassing silence, Oppressive silence, Stony silence, Ominous silence, Eerie silence, Nervous silence, Deathly silence

We need to find God, and he cannot be found in noise and restlessness. God is a friend of silence. See how nature, trees, flowers, grass-grows in silence. We need silence to be able to touch souls
- Mother Teresa

What are the internal agitations? They all come from desires, wanting something that we believe we do not have. All action follows desire: desire to have or to avoid. When there is desire we are not in the present moment. We are either in the future, imagining what it will be like to have our desire satisfied or frustrated, or we are dwelling in the past, remembering the experience of the past which was the basis for the desire. If we experienced pleasure in the past, then that memory stimulates a movement in the mind to have the experience again. Pain experienced in the past brings with it the baggage of thoughts related to avoiding the experience. In either case there is movement in the mind and therefore no stillness or silence.

There is a natural Samadhi, a total stillness, which exists in the space between the fulfilment of one desire and the beginning of the next. If we are sufficiently quiet and therefore in control of our faculties, we can resist the luring sound of desire and rest in the infinite peace within. The key is remaining in the silence and stillness of the present moment.

We have been cautioned about desire by *Krishna* in the **Bhagavad Gita:**

Know desire to be your enemy here in the world. (3:37)
When it is fed, this enemy desire inevitably leads us to careless and selfish actions, which eventually bring sorrow for everyone caught in its web. This is how the **Bhagavad Gita** describes the way we are caught by desire:

As a person contemplates the objects of sense, there arises in him attachment to them; from attachment arises desire and from desire (frustrated) anger is produced. (2.62)

From anger comes delusion; from delusion confusion of memory and loss of mindfulness; from confusion of memory and loss of mindfulness, the loss of the faculty of discrimination (Buddhi); by the loss of the faculty of discrimination, one perishes. *(2.63)*

When we are submerged in a mechanical, habitual world of attachment and desire we lose our true humanity; our integrity, wholeness, ability to love, and our capacity for self-determination.

Silence is only frightening and challenging to people who compulsively feel the need to verbalise, to manifest in the physical realm their thoughts in the form of words. The many means of communication at our disposal seem to confirm this view, although a wise observer will see that this is a hollow victory of quantity over quality. True and fine expression is greatly enhanced when it manifests naturally from silence.

In Silence there is eloquence. Stop weaving and see how the pattern improves.
- Rumi

How can we best conquer the cult of speed? The answer seems to be to learn to rest more and use quiet reflection to put aside attachments, fear, and anger. Most people ignore the valuable practice of introspection or reflection. Quick sensual gratification is the primary emphasis. Satisfaction through speed and quantity is less lasting and deep than that through silence and stillness. The main message is that in order to be most productive and effective we need the proper measure of rest and refreshment.

Some additional quotes:

We can never hear the language of the soul if our ears are filled with the loud noises of the world.
- Swami Paramanada

True silence is the rest of the mind; it is to the Spirit what sleep is to the body, nourishment and refreshment.

- *William Penn*

Soon silence will have passed into legend. Man has turned his back on silence. Day after day he invents machines and devices that increase noise and distract humanity from the essence of life, contemplation, meditation.

- *Jean Arp*

Silence is a giver; it gives some things to you! Noise is a taker; it takes some things from you! Seek for the silence!

- *Mehmet Murat ildan*

The most boring thing in the world? Silence.

- *Justin Timberlake*

These things will destroy the human race: politics without principle, progress without compassion, wealth without work, learning without silence, religion without fearlessness and worship without awareness.

- *Anthony de Mello*

And Silence, like a poultice, comes to heal the blows of sound.

- *Oliver Wendell Holmes*

An inability to stay quiet is one of the most conspicuous failings of mankind.

- *Walter Bagehot*

A quiet mind is all you need. All else will happen rightly, once your mind is quiet. In the calm and steady self-awareness inner energies wake up and work miracles on your part.

- *Nisargadatta*

The Discriminating Power of Silence: Making Decisions.

When we become aware of silence, immediately there is a state of inner still alertness and freedom. We are present in a state of unknowing. The mind is clear of any ideas or claims of knowledge. We need to learn to become at ease with the state of not knowing. This takes us beyond mind, because the mind is always trying to conclude and interpret.

When one is able to quiet the mind so that the mechanical voices of fear, doubt, and claim are silenced, then a balanced, concentrated, and fully conscious state is accessed. Decisions made in the quiet state are made without reference to my ego- based desires, but with full attention to the need of the moment. In such a state there is the possibility for a creative impulse to arise which presents the unique solution for that moment. One is fully able to discriminate and choose. It is only in the present moment that one truly exercises free will.

The more you come in contact with the inner silence, the inner emptiness, the more you have access to your intuition. Silence is the nourishment for intuition.
- Swami Dhyan Giten

In order to reach the still, quiet state of the present moment we need to learn to pause more frequently in the course of our daily physical and mental activities.

Coming to rest in the moment, dropping all tensions, doubts, worries, plans for the future etc, is a powerful discipline which leads to this greater freedom to choose. The space created gives us a sense of calm from which confidence, inspiration, and courage arise quite naturally to meet the need of the moment.

It also provides intuitive access to the well spring of spiritual and ethical insight. *Michael Smith*, author of **The Sound of Silence - How to Find Inspiration in the Age of Information,** quotes a number of other modern authors on this very topical issue.

Among those quoted is *Erik Andren,* who describes the process of making decisions based on first bringing the ever- moving mind to stillness, reflecting quietly to avail oneself of our full faculties and then deciding. He calls this: **R & D Time - Reflection & Decision Time.**

A further quote is from the Italian poet, *Rosa Bellino*, who describes the condition most conducive to the attainment of such a state:

Silence allows the muddy water of the mind to clear. Silence is the womb, the space that allows one to hear a harmony and a rhythm.

John O Donohue wrote in his book, **Anam Cara Spiritual Wisdom for the Celtic World:**

Silence is a great friend of the soul…You must make space for it so that it may begin to work for you…If you have a trust in and expectation of your own solitude, everything that you need to know will be revealed to you.

It is important that we learn to live with silence. Opportunities to practise silence are rare for those active members of the community, the householders, but as the need for greater silence is recognised, retreats for lay people i.e. not the clergy, have become more common. An increasingly popular form is a 'Silent Retreat' offered by various spiritual, religious, and self-development groups. In such programmes outward silence is observed and exercises are offered to encourage deeper inner stillness through such practices as yoga, Tai Chi, reflection, contemplation, and meditation.

Silence is both a physical and spiritual necessity for me. In the attitude of silence the soul finds the path in a clearer light and what is elusive and deceptive resolves itself into crystal clearness.
- Mahatma Gandhi

The Discriminating Power of Silence - Communicating

Communication is commonly thought of as being facilitated by an exchange of words, either spoken or written. In all cases communication involves the mental perception of words and the subsequent interpretation. Great importance is put on the understanding of words and concepts and the proper means of expression, both verbal and written.

Wise men speak because they have something to say; fools speak because they have to say something.
- Plato

We are so accustomed to relying upon words to manage and control others. If we are silent, who will take control? God will take control, but we will never let him take control until we trust him. Silence is intimately related to trust.
- Richard Foster

Key to effective communications is fine listening. If we are able to give our full attention to listening, we will be able to connect with something greater, a silence that is beyond sound, that cannot be understood through thought. When there is silence there is communication at a different level which is deeper and finer. Habitual ideas and thoughts no longer get in the way.

Silence is a better communicator than the spoken or written word. In silence prejudices and pre-conceptions fade away.
- Mahatma Gandhi

But why is it that we are so ready to chatter and gossip with each other, when we so seldom return to silence without some injury to our conscience? The reason why we are so fond of talking with each other is that we think we will find consolation in this manner and to refresh a heart worried with so many cares. And we prefer to speak and think of these things which we like and desire or of those we dislike. Alas, however all this is often of no purpose, for the outward consolation is no small obstacle to inner and divine consolation
- Thomas a'Kempis

Many of our decisions involve interaction with others, each with their own point of view and perspective. It is important that we listen carefully to what is said, to appreciate and be open to the view and the needs of others and to take this into account as part of the analysis of the situation being considered.

This careful listening is achieved only when the mind is silent, fully connected and concentrated in the moment to the sounds being spoken. These sounds carry with them more than just physical meaning; there is also a whole world of emotional content which needs to be appreciated and considered. The internal quiet creates space for the still small voice within to reveal intuitive insights which then quite naturally become the basis for our response.

All too often a quiet intuitive response is overlaid with the louder sound of a commentator, our ego- based voice, with all its conditioned responses based on past experiences and driven by the desire for a particular result.

A good example of this type of communication is that between teacher and student. Teachers who respond from this state of inner stillness in this way describe how the appropriate words seem to simply arise and are just spoken by them, with no thought or apparent effort. They just appear.

The quality and effectiveness of communications seems to be dependent on achieving a balance between the intellectual and emotional elements. One description offered regarding the process by which speech is manifest from silence says that speech begins in silence within the being. The next stage is where the sound, as yet unspoken, is experienced in the heart, in its fullness. One can hear the gravity and richness of such a sound uttered from the heart, which at the same time is also fresh and lively.

The next stage is where the mind is activated to one degree or another. If the heart and mind are in harmony then what is finally spoken by the tongue and mouth will carry a substantial presence. It carries great power and others are able to connect with the meaning at a very deep level. If the sound began only at the mental level, the effect would be different. It can also have a powerful effect, but not quite the same as when heart and mind are as one.

Some additional quotes:

In the attitude of silence the soul finds the path in a clearer light, and what is elusive and deceptive resolves itself into crystal clearness. Our life is a long and arduous quest after Truth.
- Mahatma Gandhi

Give yourself completely to the act of listening. Beyond the sounds there is something greater, a silence, a sacredness, that cannot be understood through thought.
- Eckhart Tolle

The small truth has words that are clear; the great truth has great silence.
- Rabindranath Tagore

Silence at the proper season is wisdom, and better than any speech
- Plutarch

What is so special about silence? Solitude and quiet connect you to your creative source and releases the limitless intelligence of the universe.
- Robin S Sharma

The Pause; that impressive silence, that eloquent silence, that geometrically progressive silence which often achieves a desired effect where no combination of words, however so felicitous, could accomplish it.
-*Mark Twain*

He who does not understand your silence will probably not understand your words.
- *Elbert Hubbard*

Does not everything depend on our interpretation of the silence around us?
- *Lawrence Durrell*

Blessed is the man who, having nothing to say, abstains from giving us wordy evidence of the fact.
- *George Eliot*

Under all speech that is good for anything there lies a silence that is better.
- *Thomas Carlyle*

There is something hugely civilised about allowing long pauses in a conversation. Very few people can stand that kind of silence.
- *James Robertson*

In human intercourse the tragedy begins, not when there is misunderstanding about words, but when silence is not understood.
- *Henry David Thoreau*

In the End, we will remember not the words of our enemies, but the silence of our friends.
- *Martin Luther King, Jr*

Silence is the source of healing.
- *Swami Dhyan Giten*

Keep silence for the most part, and speak only when you must, and then briefly.
- Epictetus

Lying is done with words and also with silence.
- Adrienne Rich

There are those among you who seek the talkative through fear of being alone. The silence of aloneness reveals to their eyes their naked selves and they would escape. And there are those who talk, and without knowledge or forethought reveal a truth which they themselves do not understand. And there are those who have the truth within them, but they tell it not in words.
In the bosom of such as these the spirit dwells in rhythmic silence.
- Kahlil Gibran

Language can only deal meaningfully with a special, restricted segment of reality. The rest, and it is presumably the much larger part, is silence.
- George Steiner,

Be silent or let thy words be worth more than silence.
- Pythagoras

Nothing strengthens authority so much as silence.
- Leonardo da Vinci

Silence is one of the great arts of conversation.
- Cicero

Perhaps the most important thing we bring to another person is the silence in us, not the sort of silence that is filled with unspoken criticism or hard withdrawal. The sort of silence, that is a place of refuge, of rest, of acceptance of someone as they are. We are all hungry for this other silence. It is hard to find. In its presence we can remember something beyond the moment, a strength on which to build a life. Silence is a place of great power and healing.
-Rachel Naomi Remen

I have learned silence from the talkative, tolerance from the intolerant, and kindness from the unkind; yet strangely, I am ungrateful to these teachers.
- *Kahlil Gibran*

Silence is more eloquent than words
- *Thomas Carlyle*

The world would be happier if men had the same capacity to be silent that they have to speak
- *Baruch Spinoza*

I often regret that I have spoken; never that I have been silent
- *Publiliu Syrus*

When the eagles are silent the parrots begin to jabber.
- *Winston Churchill*

That man's silence is wonderful to listen to.
- *Thomas Hardy*

Our safest eloquence concerning Him is our silence.
- *Richard Hooker*

In not only the physical silence, but in the real mental silence, the wisdom dawns.
- *Swami Satchidananda*

Silence builds anticipation and the perfected herald of joy
- *Shakespeare (Much Ado About Nothing)*

Silence, the unique language, ever surging in the Heart, is the state of grace.
- *Sri Ramana Maharshi*

The Creative Power of Silence - Music

Music is a wonderful example of measured silence and sound. All music emerges from silence, to which sooner or later it must return. At its simplest, we may conceive of music as the relationship between sounds and the silence that surrounds them. Silence is considered by some to be an imaginary state in which all sounds are absent; akin perhaps to the infinity of time and the space that surrounds us. We cannot ever hear utter silence, nor can we fully imagine such concepts as infinity and eternity. When we create music, we express life. But the source of music is silence, which is the ground of our musical being, the fundamental note of life. How we make music depends on our relationship with silence.

Great attention was paid not only to the notes but also the space between the notes and the phrases. This was an important reminder of the stillness behind the

demanding activity of playing and singing. When this became the point from which the music was heard, the inner qualities and vitality of the music became more apparent and delightful.
- *Leon MacLaren*

After silence, that which comes nearest to expressing the inexpressible is music.
- *Aldous Huxley*

Music is the silence between the notes.
- *Claude Debussy*

Music is pleasing not only because of the sound but because of the silence that is in it: without the alternation of sound and silence there would be no rhythm.
- *Thomas Merton*

Here are some comments on silence by current musicians taken from: **The Power of Silence**, *by Graham Turner:*

Silence is the canvas upon which the whole thing (music) is painted.
- *Stephen Varcoe*

The silence before and after a performance are an integral part of any piece of music. The piece starts before the first note is played. A great performer will know instinctively the exact moment at which the music is meant to start.
- *Mark Messenger*

Silence properly felt and understood takes an audience deeper into the meaning of a work than do the notes. Performers are actually aware of their audience. They are aware of them because of the quality of the silence when they are playing.
- *Roger Vignoles*

If there is no reverence for silence the music would be dead, it would just be continuous noise.
- *Julian Jacobson*

By its very nature, silence calls forth reflection. That's the reason why it is so potent. Music is not all about sound.
- David Ward

Here are two quotes from *Jean-Philippe Calvin* on the subject of silence in the religious music of the Middle Ages, one describing aspects of Gregorian Chant and the other on a similar pattern in Eastern music.

Gregorian Chant - After each phrase there was a very deliberate pause, so that the text could be reflected on, so that the memory of it could seep into the soul.

In Chinese and Japanese music of the same period, somewhat influenced by the philosophy of Zen, there were even longer and more meaningful silences.

There are many types of silence. There is a silence before the note, there is a silence at the end and there is a silence in the middle
- Daniel Barenboim

Music and silence combine strongly because music is done with silence, and silence is full of music.
- Marcel Marceau

The hymn, *O Still Small Voice of Calm*, written by Charles Wesley, is a very fine example of a piece of music which, in both the beauty of the melody and the relevance of the words, opens the heart to the importance of silence. Here are some excerpts:

> O Sabbath rest by Galilee!
> O calm of the hills above,
> Where Jesus knelt to share with thee
> the silence of eternity
> interpreted by love,
> interpreted by love.
>
> Drop thy still dews in quietness,
> Till all our strivings cease;
> Take from our souls the strain and stress,
> and let our ordered lives confess
> the beauty of thy peace,
> the beauty of thy peace.
>
> Breathe through the heats of our desire
> thy coolness and thy balm;
> Let sense be dumb, let flesh retire;
> Speak through the earthquake,
> wind and fire,
> O still, small voice of calm,
> O still, small voice of calm.

Pachelbel's Canon
lu - ya, Al - le - lu - ya,
lu - ya, Al - le - lu - ya,
lu - ya, Al - le - lu - ya,
Musica

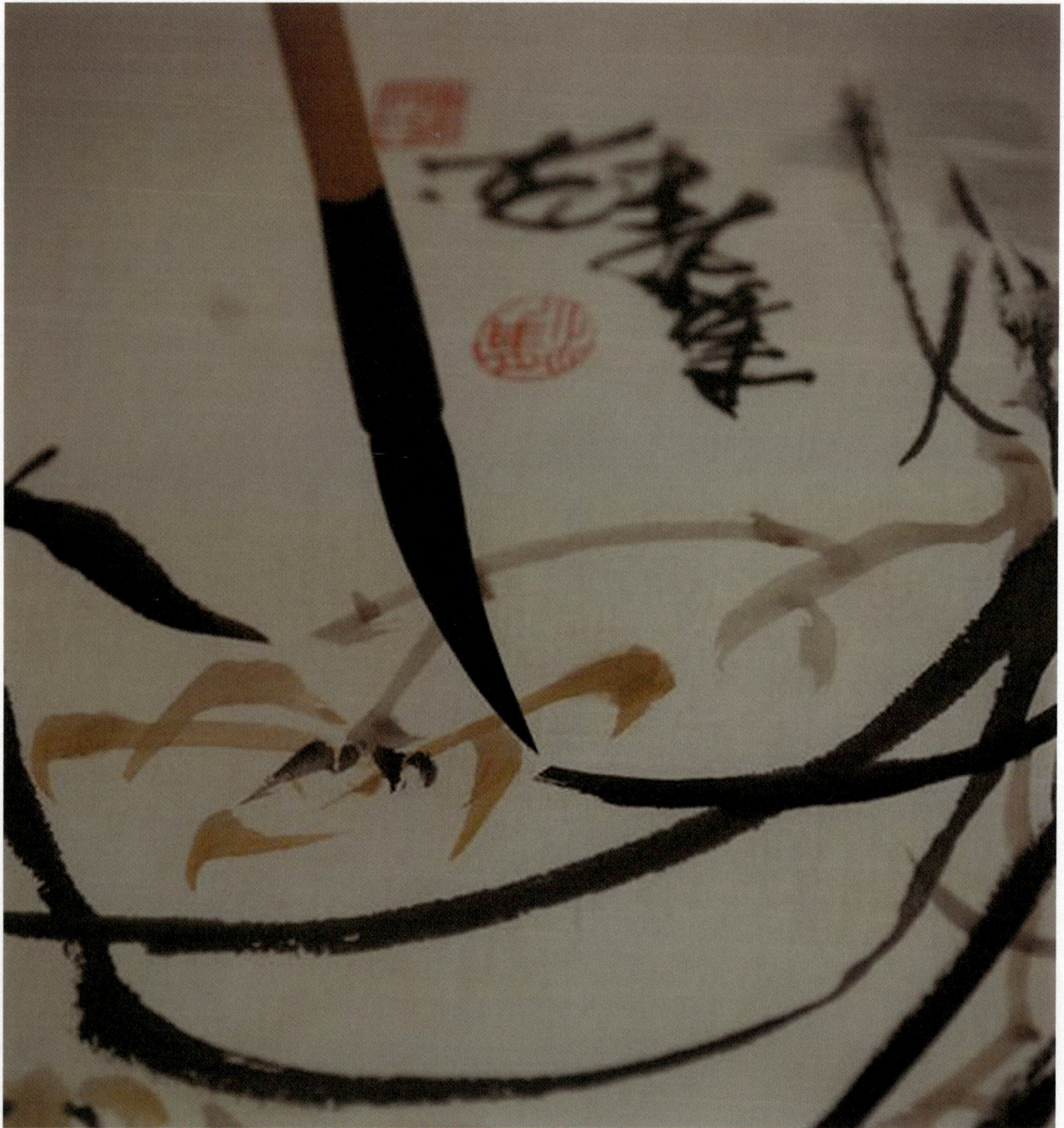

Silence and The Great Spiritual Teachers

Many great sages and teachers sought the tranquility and solace of silence as an example for us to learn from and to follow:

- Lao Tzu in the caves of the mountains of China
- Muhammad in a cave of Mt Hira
- Buddha meditating on the banks of the Nairanyana river
- Jesus alone in the wilderness for 40 days

Lao Tzu in the caves of the mountains in China

Lao Tzu, an older contemporary of Confucius, lived in the 6th century BC, and is the founder of Taoism. The conjectured years of his life are 604-531 BC. This legendary Taoist philosopher, whose name can be translated as the Old Master, for a time lived a life of silence and solitude in caves in the mountains of China. When he emerged he wrote a manual of self-cultivation and government, as well as a metaphorical account of reality, called Daodejing (a.k.a. Tao Te Ching) and translated as "Book of the Way and Its Power.

Lao Tzu recommended withdrawal from the values of a materialistic society and a retreat into the wisdom and values of the inner self.Desires cause harmful relationships between the self and others and lead people to inappropriate things for their own satisfaction. Desires are evoked by the attractiveness and variety of things.

Lao Tzu counselled people to make their desires negligible, to minimise their personal interests, to limit and diminish the ego, and to return the self to a state of simple contentment. He denounced the gratification of one's appetites and senses and the search for wealth and status. Those who live according to their true being and nature will seek inner peace and creative quietude and will act through freedom from desires, and through selflessness, softness, moderation, and openness to all things.

Muhammad in a cave on Mount Hira

It is known that for some time Muhammad used to retire to Mount Hira outside Mecca to contemplate the meaning of life in undisturbed solitude. Here he was able to reflect and question, without fear of social retribution, the beliefs of his own people. Down below he was accustomed to a bustling society where hundreds of people from all over Arabia mixed with each other in their daily lives. That, to any ordinary man, was the simple reality of life. The universe above and the earth below had no real relevance apart from the incessant activity of human and other forms of life on the surface of the earth.

High up on Mount Hira, as he searched the broad, silent horizons before him, things began to appear to be somewhat different to the seeker who, although in the prime of his life at the age of forty years, had determined to seek the true meaning of his existence. As he scanned the horizon, however, he must have been impressed rather with an immense serenity, a tranquil silence stretching into the heavens in a realm far beyond the human scope of perception.

About the year 610 Muhammad had a vision in which he was called on to preach the message entrusted to him by God. Further revelations came to him intermittently over the remaining years of his life, and these revelations constitute the text of the Qu'ran. At first in private and then publicly, Muhammad began to proclaim his message: that there is but one God and that Muhammad is his messenger sent to warn people of the Judgement Day and to remind them of God's goodness.

Today the pilgrimage to Mecca is carried out in silence as it is believed that the silence will help make a connection with Allah. In silence Allah speaks to you. 500 verses of the Qu'ran say that we need to reflect/contemplate/ponder on the things of creation including ourselves. This process is aided by silence.

Buddha meditating on the banks of the Niranjana river

For a long time Buddha retired to a solitary existence and a practice of meditation under a chosen tree. The day finally came when he declared that his mystical search for truth had finally yielded its light – all life and its trials could be resolved in one proverb, he proclaimed. Desire was the cause of all suffering; subdue your own personal desires and longings and then pain and suffering will have no effect or meaning.

Before his enlightenment the Buddha too spent extended periods alone in the forests. Reminiscing on this time many years later, he said: **'Such was my seclusion that I would plunge into some forest and live there. If I saw a cowherd, shepherd, grass-cutter, wood-gatherer or forester, I would flee so that they would not see me or me them.'** Even after attaining enlightenment he would occasionally go into solitude. In the **Samyutta Nikaya** he said:

'I wish to go into solitude for half a month. No one is to come to see me except the one who brings my food.'

The Buddha made a distinction between physical and psychological solitude and considered the first to be more important. For him, psychological solitude meant isolating the mind from negative thoughts and emotions. The Buddha recognized that people can choose to be solitary for a variety of reasons, some positive, others less so. It is certainly true that regular periods of solitude, and even occasional extended periods, can be psychologically refreshing. It can teach independence, rest the mind, enhance an appreciation of silence and provide the opportunity to have a good look at oneself.

Some observations of the Buddha :

'Monks, apply yourselves to solitude. One who does so will see things as they are.'

'His thought is quiet, quiet are his words and deeds, when he has obtained the freedom of true knowledge, when he has become a quiet man.'

Jesus alone in the wilderness for 40 days

What motivated Jesus to spend 40 days and nights of solitude, prayer, and fasting in the Judean wilderness? This desert landscape was largely uninhabitable and was full of dangers for anyone who dared to venture in it for long: danger from scorching heat by day and extreme cold by night, danger from wild animals and scorpions, plus the scarcity of food and water.

For God's chosen people of Israel and many of their leaders, the desert was a place of testing, encounter, and renewal. When the Israelites were freed from slavery in Egypt, they wandered 40 years in the wilderness. This was seen as a time of purification and preparation for entry into the Promised Land. Moses went to the mountain of the Lord in the Sinai wilderness and stayed there for 40 days and nights in prayer and fasting. Elijah, after he was fed with bread from heaven, journeyed through the wilderness without any food for 40 days to the mountain of God. Jesus was without any food in the wilderness for 40 days to prepare himself for the mission that the Father had sent him to accomplish.

Why did Jesus choose such a barren, lonely place for an intense and long period of prayer and fasting? Matthew, Mark, and Luke tell us in their gospel accounts that Jesus was led by the Holy Spirit into the wilderness. Mark states it most emphatically: *"The Spirit immediately drove him out into the wilderness"***(Mark 1:12).** What compelled Jesus to seek solitude away from his family and friends for such a lengthy period? Was it simply to test himself and prepare for his mission?

Or was he also allowing himself to be tempted by Satan? The word tempt in English usually means to entice someone to do what is wrong or forbidden. The scriptural word used here also means to test in the sense of proving and purifying someone to see if they are ready for the task at hand. When Christ overcame the three temptations of Satan, he then moved confidently to fulfil his role in guiding his people to their salvation.

Religious Silence - The Christian Monastic Tradition

In the world of religion and philosophy the practice of silence plays a vital part. It creates a substance, an atmosphere, a space, a state of being that enables the seeker to find access to an inner sanctuary entirely covered over by the restless concerns of the physical and mental worlds. It is within this inner realm, which is considered to be the spiritual realm, that true meaning and understanding is to be found.

Here are some excerpts from **Into the Silent Land** *by Martin Laird:*

To contemplate is to quietly concentrate thought on a subject, especially spiritual matters, to meditate. The word comes from the Latin com –intensive + templum-open space. That space is where the subject is to be found.

In the Christian tradition the aim of contemplation is communion with God. Communion with God in the silence of the heart is a God-given capacity like the rhododendron's capacity to flower, the fledgling's for flight, and the child's natural expression of joy.

This communion and the way to achieve it are described in many ways in Christian scripture:

Be still and know that I am God.
- Psalm 46

Even a fool, when he holds his peace, is counted wise; and he that shutteth his lips is esteemed as a man of understanding
- Proverbs

That which we most require for our spiritual growth is the silence of desire and of the tongue before God, who is so high that the only language He hears is the silent language of love.
- St John of the Cross

This communion with the Lord cannot be reduced to a spiritual technique. The practice of silent contemplation simply prepares the ground for something to take place. An analogy is of a gardener who does not actually grow plants, but simply prepares the ground for a natural process to take place. The natural process in terms of communion is to remove the coverings that hide the union, the unity that is pre-existent. The unity or communion is the natural state but the experience of it is covered over, primarily by the movements of the mental and emotional realm. Silence begins with an outer silence which then deepens to include an interior silence as well. There are two contemplative practices of fundamental importance in the Christian tradition: the practice of silence, stillness, also called meditation, still prayer, contemplative prayer and the practice of watchfulness or awareness.

The very best and utmost attainment in this life is to remain still and let God speak in thee. In silence a man can most readily preserve his integrity
- *Meister Eckhart*

Silence, solitude and prayer are the most important elements in monastic life.
- *Thomas Merton*

In silence and quietness the devout soul makes progress and learns the hidden mysteries of the scriptures.
- *Ecclesiastes*

Prayer is about brevity, simplicity and trust and the natural completion of these is silence.
- *Fr Laurence Freeman*

When the mind comes into its own stillness and enters the silent land, the sense of separation goes. Union is seen to be the fundamental reality and separateness a highly filtered mental perception. For when the mind is brought to stillness and all our claims and strategies of acquisition are dropped, a deeper truth presents itself.

For God alone my soul in silence waits..
- *Psalm 62:1*

The further I advance in solitude, the more clearly I see the goodness of things.
- *Thomas Merton*

Those who sound alarms regarding the contemplative path as being anti-community reveal a shocking ignorance of the simple fact: that the journey to union with God is singular and all- embracing. Communion with God and communion with others are realisations of the same Source.

God far exceeds all words that we can here express. In silence he is heard, in silence he is worshipped best.
- *Angelus Silesius*

If you love truth, be a lover of silence. Silence, like sunlight, will illuminate you in God and deliver you from the phantoms of ignorance.
- Isaac of Nineveh (7th cent Bishop & Theologian)

In the monasteries the monk's deepest language comes from the depth of silence. The word monk comes from the Greek word meaning alone. St Anthony, the first of the Desert Fathers withdrew into the Egyptian desert in 285AD. He sought a life of solitude, poverty, obedience, silence, and prayer in order to dispose the soul for intimate connection with God. The practice grew, and by 394 there were 22,000 monks in the area under similar disciplines.

In 527 St Benedict, who spent some years in silence and solitude in a cave in Subiaco, founded a monastery in Italy which combined the Roman contributions of order and discipline with the traditional rules of poverty, chastity, and obedience. The Benedictine order is still in existence today, practising what became known as the Rule of Benedict.

The monastic movement was the great healer for Europe. It was the silence of monasticism that enabled the development of an inner strength and confidence founded on the principles of Christianity which burst forth on the scene in Europe in the 13th and 14th centuries in a movement which was later to be named Renaissance – a re-birth.

Here are some words from a member of a current monastic order, *Father Richard Rohr*, a Franciscan friar, as described in **The Power of Silence.**

To experience silence you have to let go of all your attachments-your ego. Jesus said, 'Unless you die to yourself…'

We do not realise how much we substitute the mind, which works with words, for Reality. True silence does not evaluate, it simply values.

Emphasis in Christian meditation is in hearing the inner voice speaking, for to us this is the indwelling presence of the Holy Spirit.

The sickness is superficiality. When you go to the depth of anything you will meet God-through direct experience.

Some additional quotes:

The true contemplative is not one who prepares his mind for a particular message that he wants or expects to hear, but is one who remains empty because he knows that he can never expect to anticipate the words that will transform his darkness into light. He does not even anticipate a special kind of transformation. He does not demand light instead of darkness. He waits on the Word of God in silence, and, when he is answered it is not so much by a word that bursts into his silence. It is by his silence itself, suddenly, inexplicably revealing itself to him as a word of great power, full of the voice of God.
- Thomas Merton

Every Great spiritual tradition has known that the human spirit begins to be aware of its own Source only in profound stillness.
- Fr John Main

The easiest way to get touch with this universal power is through silent Prayer. Shut your eyes, shut your mouth, and open your heart. This is the golden rule of prayer. Prayer should be soundless words coming forth from the centre of your heart filled with love
- Amit Ray

Keep silence before me, O islands; and let the people renew their strength: let them come near; then let them speak: let us come near together to judgment.
- Isaiah 41:1

Religious Silence - The Vedic Spiritual Tradition

Here is a view according to the Indian Vedic tradition showing how the spiritual realm relates to the sensory world. These aspects describe the act of creation, where the unlimited becomes limited at three levels:

SPIRITUAL	CAUSAL	SUBTLE	PHYSICAL
(Source/Substance)	(Cause)	(Subtle Body/Mind)	(Physical Body)

Within the creation, Sound is the causal form, Thought the subtle form and Words and their Meaning are the physical form. Words are created from sound for the purpose of communication.

SILENCE	SOUND	THOUGHT	WORD/MEANING
(Unlimited)		(The Limited Creation of 3 levels)	

The Sanskrit names for these four levels of speech as described in the Vedic tradition are: Paraa (Source), Pasyanti (Causal), Madhyamaa (Subtle), Vaikhari (Physical).

The unlimited cannot be bound. Usually it is not accessible to ordinary man, so he has to realise it although he already has it. In the common worldly way one only works through Madyhamaa and Vaikhari. To go deeper and to experience the centres of Pasyanti and Paraa, it would be necessary to shut out the other two as much as possible. This again is possible at a high level of consciousness.
- Sri Shantananda Saraswati

In this Vedic tradition the creation is composed of three elements or qualities: the creative quality   called Rajas, the sustaining element, Sattva, and the dissolving phase, Tamas. We observe their working in all aspects of life; there is birth,

sustained life, and then dissolution or death. With regard to silence one needs to be careful not to confuse the idea of true silence and stillness, which is the element of Sattva, with dullness, inertia and inaction, known as Tamas.

True silence impacts the body, mind, and our emotional centre, making us finer instruments for efficient, concentrated and compassionate work.

All other knowledge is only petty and trivial knowledge; the experience of silence alone is the real and perfect knowledge. True teaching is through silence which is the state without thoughts –it is the only real state.
- *Ramana Maharshi*

The nearer you approach to God, the less you reason and argue. When you attain Him, then all sounds, all reasoning and disputing come to an end. Then you go into Samadhi, into communion with God in silence.
- *Sri Ramakrishna*

How sweet is the sound of silence! How tender is its touch! How fragrant is its breathing! How lovely is its form! O be still yet awhile that my soul may see and feel, hear and touch its own realm of peace divine.
- *Swami Paramananda*

He who is indifferent to blame or praise, who is silent, content with anything, without attachment, steady- minded, full of devotion; this man is dear to Me.
- *Bhagavad Gita 12:19*

Here is part of a conversation between *Yoga Vasistha* and *Lord Rama* from the **Supreme Yoga:**

Yoga Vasistha: **When one thoroughly investigates all this, it is clearly seen that the pure consciousness alone exists and nothing else. It is beyond description .At the end of the investigation utter silence alone remains. Though engaged in all activities, it remains unaffected like space, as if it were dumb. The enlightened one therefore attains the knowledge of the infinite and remains utterly silent. He is the best among men. They who know the truth realise that it is neither real nor unreal; hence they** realise the truth as silence. What is seen here as the objective universe is in truth the Supreme Brahman. The ocean, the mountain, the clouds, earth, all the unborn and uncreated, the entire universe exists in Brahman as the Great Silence.

Lord Rama: When one has realised the supreme truth, what does he become?

Yoga Vasistha: To such a one even the rocks become friends and the trees in the forest are relations, even when he lives in the middle of a forest the very animals become his kith and kin....Disharmony becomes harmony, sorrow is great joy and even when engaged in intense activity he experiences deep silence.

Yoga Vasistha: Now, O Rama please tell me how you realise that this world, though it seems to be real, is non-existent.

Lord Rama: Whatever is, is. That which is, is clear as the sky, full as the centre of a rock, silent and peaceful as the stone and infinite. Such is the creation. For this creation exists in the pure, infinite consciousness which is the reality of all thoughts and concepts

Yoga Vasistha: This supreme truth is established only in total silence, not by logic, discussion and argumentation.

Here are three more relevant quotes:

It is raining and you can hear the patter of the drops. You can hear it with your ears, or you can hear it out of that deep silence. If you hear it with complete silence of the mind, then the beauty of it is such that cannot be put into words or onto canvas, because that beauty is something beyond self-expression.
- *Krishnamurti*

The quiet mind is all you need. All else will happen rightly once your mind is quiet. In calm and steady self-awareness inner energies wake up and work miracles on your part.
- *Nisargadatta*

It is when we silence the chattering of our mind that we can truly hear what is in our heart and find the still, clear purity that lies within the soul. Spiritual love carries us into the silence of our original state of being. This silence contains the power to create harmony in all relationships and the sweetness to sustain them. And it is when I am silent within that I can let God into my heart and mind, filling me with peace, love and power.

- Dadi Janki

Religious Silence - The Quaker Tradition

Quakerism arose in the second-half of seventeenth-century England initially as a group of non- conformists who rejected the established ritual and dogma in favour of a minimal statement of Christian belief. Quakerism has always been about the individual and community on the one hand and social service on the other. Service is not offered as a duty, but from the fullness of conviction in the example and teachings of Jesus. The Quaker framework for individual and community is silence.

Silence in worship consists of participants (no longer necessarily Quakers today) sitting in a circle at a private home or agreed place in "meeting." There is no church, no minister, no ritual, liturgy, or recitation. Usually set for about an hour, anyone may speak if so moved, but the expectation is that any vocalisation is not frivolous.

Each made it their work to return inwardly to the measure of grace in themselves, and not being only silent as to words, but even abstaining from all their own thoughts, imaginations and desires.
- Robert Barclay

The goals of silence are attentiveness to ordinary life, rejection of false consolations of worship, and recognition of the will of God.
- John Woolman

The modern Quaker writer Arthur O Roberts, nicely outline the characteristics of silence in his book *Devotions on Silence:*

1. fosters awe before the Almighty;
2. indicates submission to God;
3. provides a posture for worship;
4. provides freedom from noise and distraction;
5. is the condition for tranquility;
6. sets the stage for prayer;
7. signifies respect for others;
8. renews wonder at the world;
9. provides holy space;
10. prepares for effective social witness.

Silent Retreats & Silence - My Experience

As was noted in the Introduction my interest and appreciation of silence began when I was 18 years old and my uncle invited me to join him on a silent weekend retreat run in a local Jesuit monastery. The retreat was attended by about 100 men of all ages. It turned out that I was the youngest of the lot. My experience on that first weekend of the power of silence to bring about a sense of real peace and contentment, as well as clarity of mind, convinced me that such an activity was something of great value and that I should go again next year. I did so for the next 11 years until the time that I left the US to live in Europe.

A day at the monastery began for us with a Mass where the priest offered some 'points for meditation', as they were called. This was a very short sermon in which an aspect of the Christian teaching was offered up for us to consider and reflect upon during the day. We then had breakfast, in silence. On the first day I was slightly uncomfortable about not speaking at all, even to ask someone to pass an item of food. As it turned out such practical aspects of having a meal together seemed to happen quite naturally as an atmosphere of service was created so that we all tried to be aware of and to anticipate the needs of others. This was very satisfying as was the opportunity to taste the food more fully.

It was clear from the beginning that an excellent use of the quiet time was for self-examination. I considered what had happened over the past year, exploring my responses to the play of creation as it was presented to me. After a while it was as if I was observing activities from a distance, without claim or judgement. At the time of the first retreat I was just into my 2nd year as a university student studying for a degree in electrical engineering.

Something happened in this person's life a few months after this initial retreat, which I am not sure I can attribute to my brief introduction to silence, but it may have influenced it. When I graduated from high school in 1960 there was a great demand for engineers in the US. The advice given to me by my school was that with my interest and capabilities in mathematics, I should study engineering and probably electrical engineering which involved lots of maths. And so I followed that direction.

I really enjoyed my first year of study at New Jersey Institute of Technology (then called Newark College of Engineering). It was demanding program, classes from 9:00am until 5:00pm every day, with 3-4 hours of homework each evening and a good deal more work on the weekends. Despite the heavy workload I really enjoyed the study as there was in fact a considerable amount of mathematics and physics in the first year curriculum.

As we entered our 2nd year we were told that we would be gradually exposed to the more practical side of electrical engineering in the form of laboratory experiments. A short time after my retreat weekend our class was brought into a huge laboratory complete with a number of large machines, generators, power supplies etc. We were shown around the lab and it was explained that as engineers we would become very familiar with the workings of all this equipment and how it is used in industry.

We were free to look around and at one point a found myself standing alone looking around the room. I became very still within and then with great clarity of mind the following direction was heard, '*This engineering path is not for me. I do not want to work with machines. I want to work with people. I will however stay with this study because a technical degree is very valued today, but my real education will begin later.*' I can still hear the echo of the last statement-'*my real education will begin later.*' It certainly has worked out that way.

The retreats attended during my time at university continued to be beneficial in enabling me to get taste of the peace and clarity that can be experienced when we learn to be quiet. Quieting the mind is greatly helped by first eliminating physical speech which allows the mental world to settle more easily. This yearly reminder helped me make better use of my time at university which were very important in helping me to establish as personal self-confidence to be ready and able to meet the inevitable challenges of a very dynamic world. The 1960's were a time of great change which young people at the time could sense, but we not sure where it was heading.

Attendance at the yearly retreat became a **must do** in my schedule and all other activities were put aside for that weekend. The pattern continued and over the years, even when I left university and found employment with a computer company in Philadelphia about 100 miles from my parent's home and the retreat centre.

Two events during the period of these retreats stand out in my memory. The usual pattern for the weekend was that after an initial quieting down period, I became very still and clear by Saturday afternoon. One year, late Saturday afternoon I found that something wasn't quite right. There were still a lot of thoughts running through the mind and a sense of uncertainty and agitation was experienced. I paused for a while and then decided to read the notes I had written so far about the events of the past year. To my surprise I found that I had only written about the good things that had happened. What was missing was the important acknowledgement of those instances where I acted in a way that was not quite right, or good or useful. That was one of the blessings of such a period of silent reflection i.e. that you could learn from your mistakes as well as from positive activities like study. This must be why Socrates said that 'An unexamined life is not worth living.'

After a brief pause and prayer I took out a clean sheet of paper and took on the assignment to write down those actions over the past year that in some way I regretted. An hour later I had filled 1 ½ pages with items. The response to this list was not one of depression or grief, but of relief that I was able to objectively observe and acknowledge poor behaviour. What was useful about such an honest assessment was that the knowledge of what would have been a better response also arose quite naturally. I saw more clearly the negative impact of allowing the ego to run the show. By that I mean my unique set of likes and dislikes, preferences and ideas i.e. me, that can all to easily cover up what is really happening and what is really needed. In future sessions I became more convinced about the negative impact of allowing the noisy mind to cover over the reality of the moment which gave further confirmation of the need to embrace external and eventually inner silence.

As I reached my teenage years in the 1950's I had a string sense that anything was possible. In the US at the time all the doors were open, opportunities abounded. At the same I also recognised that I was living in an highly competitive environment where there was extensive pressure to succeed; to win in sports, to get top marks in school, to be popular and later to make lots of money in business. Losing means that you are less of a person. I gradually saw that along with the strong desire to win, there was a tendency to cover over or deny one's failings, and also to focus on the faults of others in an attempt to justify one's own position. My silent retreats helped me to become more aware of this subtle pressure to succeed and strengthened the resolve to avoid it.

I was also reminded by the sage advice on the subject contained in the poem **IF** by **Rudyard Kipling,** which was a great inspiration for me, one that helped keep me on track over the years. One of the most oft repeated lines is:

'If you can treat triumph and disaster, those two imposters just the same…'

The other incident on the silent retreat occurred when I was 23 years old. I used to keep a file of the notes I had written each year. When I had made my decision to accept a job offer to work in Brussels for my company, part of the preparations for the big move was for me to go through all my belongings to decide what was necessary to take. I decided to take my collection of retreat notes.

When I had settled in my new home in Brussels, I thought it would be a good idea to review these notes. What I discovered in the notes written in my 23rd year was a statement, *'You will live and work in Europe by the time you are 30 years old.'* There I was sitting in a house in Brussels, having arrived just 3 months shy of my 30th birthday. I had not kept that statement in mind over the years, using it as the basis for a grand plan, but I do remember the great clarity and confidence that seemed to be present when it was written.

My arrival in Brussels was the beginning of a new phase of life. Within two months of my arrival I saw an advert in a local magazine for a course in Philosophy-in English. I decided that this would be a good way to meet some new people as well as to broaden my educational horizons. It certainly accomplished both of those aims. Over the years many of the fellow students in the school became part of an extended family for me. In fact, one of my best friends in Brussels, a delightful Dutch lady called Judica, later became Mrs Palmarozza.

The Brussels School of Philosophy, as it was called, was a branch of an organisation based in London, The School of Economic Science, which was founded in 1937 to discover and live the natural laws governing man and society. The schools initial emphasis was Economics, but in the early 1960s there was a movement towards understanding more about man's nature i.e. Philosophy. Both the Christian and Platonic views were explored in some depth along with expositions on a blend of eastern and western philosophies from 2 modern philosophers, Gurdieff and Ouspensky. In the 1960's, along with the Beatles, the school became interested in Meditation and eventually adopted it as regular practice. The leader of the school then began a series of very useful meetings with a spiritual teacher in India, one of the leaders of the Indian Advaita tradition - Advaita meaning Unity.

What evolved was a system of practical philosophy which, while espousing very fine principles about our nature and our role in this creation, asked that we do not simply accept what we hear, but try to put the theory into practice in our daily lives. The school expanded rapidly and soon branches were opened by enthusiastic students in North America, Australia, New Zealand, South Africa, Ireland and several European countries, as well as in many cities in the England and Scotland.

On the first evening of the course I attended in Brussels we were given a simple exercise to connect the mind fully with each of the senses and to observe that if this was practiced, the mind naturally became quieter and more still. I remember clearly the first time this was tried. The mind did come to rest, to that same quiet state that I had grown to appreciate during my silent retreats. I decided then that this practical approach to philosophy was one that I wanted to follow.

In this period of the early 1970's Brussels was a very dynamic place with people from all over Europe and North America converging at the home of an expanding Common Market. Our philosophy classes had people from a wide range of nationalities and for someone from America who had previously made only brief holiday excursions abroad, this was another aspect of my expanding education. One of the economics courses that I attended had people from 9 different countries participating. It was fascinating to hear their different perspectives and also reassuring to hear that on certain matters of principles and law, we were in full agreement.

I continued to attend classes for my entire period of 8 years that I lived in Brussels. After about 2 years I took up a system of Meditation which I found to be the finest most consistent way to connect with my inner silence. I began to realise that the silence and peace are always there and that the need was to quiet the moving active mind and to merge with it.

There were a number of other courses offered in the Brussels school. I joined a music group in order to overcome my very firmly held idea that 'I cannot sing'. I began a course in calligraphy, the art of beautiful writing, which I still practice today and I studied Vedic Mathematics a very fine system of mathematics that was just being rediscovered after a long period of hibernation. I joined a group of people reading the Dialogues of Plato and to my surprise began the study of the Sanskrit language, which I later discovered is the source of all the major Indo-European languages i.e. Greek , Latin, English, German etc, etc. My real education had definitely begun.

One of the most significant discoveries of this time in Brussels occurred in my 3rd year. No one in the school was paid. We were all volunteers and all the functions were performed by the students, including the function of teaching the classes. One day I was asked by the leader of the school if I would be interested in teaching an entry level class, Part 1 as it was known. Something in me went very quiet. I agreed and was given an excellent briefing by the school leader on the way to conduct a class of students new to the philosophic teaching we were offering.

On the evening of the first class I sat alone in the classroom awaiting the arrival of the first students. I had a very strong feeling that a good deal of my life was a preparation for this moment. It felt so right. I have continued in that role as a teacher/tutor of philosophy in the school for 40 years.

During that period I have discovered that maintaining an inner quiet is the key to effective teaching. By being present in the moment, listening carefully to your own voice and the voice of the student, the right response seems to just arise, from you know not where. You become like a fine instrument though which a beautiful song is played. For me it has been a great honour to be able to serve in this role.

The school also organised yearly philosophy retreats and sometimes we travelled to the UK to participate with members of the main school based in London. At these retreats, in addition to study and practical activities, there were two periods of meditation each day, quiet reflective activities and on occasion, periods of silence for which I was most grateful.

When my employer abruptly announced in 1979 that they would be closing the Brussels office and moving all the staff to Minneapolis, Minnesota from which they would run the European operation, I was faced with a stark choice. When I joined the company in 1964 there were about 2,700 employees. At time of this announcement, 15 years later, there were 35-40,000 employees and I held quite a high position as General Manager of one of the European businesses.

All I could do was to go off on my own silent retreat in my home and reflect on the next step. No one could really advise me. It was a decision that would have to come from within. At some point an idea arose in mind. I had launched a new business in Europe based on the use of computers in education and training. The founder of my company has this vision about how computers in time would be used extensively in the field of education and training. After some consideration and reflection I shared this vision.

It then came to me that in order to be able to properly manifest this vision, I would need to know more about Education, its principles, history and its current state.

Coincidently a friend of mine told me about an excellent one year education studies programme at Oxford University and suggested I write them. So I wrote a letter to them saying that I did not know much about education, but I did understand the new technologies of the day and expressing a desire to explore how they might be effectively used in education. I was not confident of a positive response.

What became a game-changer was that this Oxford Education Studies Department also received, at the same time, a letter from the UK Department of Education asking if they might be able to help advise on a new Computer-Assisted Learning policy that was being developed. As a result of this coincidence I was invited for an interview.

The Oxford Professor of Education who interviewed me was a keen Platonist and we connected nicely with each other. As a result I was accepted in the programme which was also attended by a group of Heads and Deputy Heads who were spending a sabbatical year studying for a Special Diploma in Educational Studies. The idea was that I would have a chance to explain and demonstrate to this group of experienced educationalists what was possible with the technology and then to discuss with them how such tools could be most effectively used in schools.

When I presented this option to my company, they said that they could arrange for me to take a similar course in a university in Minneapolis. They would not accept the Oxford option and so the choice was to either go back to the US to live and work OR leave the company, move to the UK, spend a year studying Education- at my own expense and then who knows what?

By now the practices of Meditation and reflection had been sufficiently well established that I was able to quietly consider the possibilities. After a period of silent reflection it became clear that I needed to take a step into the unknown and accept the Oxford offer. I did so and then doors seemed to magically open for me.

I still had a final period of work with my company who agreed to allow me to work for them in London, at a much reduced salary, until the time that course began in September. While on a business trip to Israel I told the manager of that office about my decision. He asked me where I would live in London and I said that I did not have a clue. He said, 'I own a flat in a place called Highgate, in north London, which has just become available.' Thus in a flash part of my accommodation needs were solved.

The other issue was where would I live during the time of study in Oxford? While on a visit to the UK over that summer I attended an art festival that the London school organised each year at Waterperry House and Gardens near Oxford. The estate consisted of a beautiful stately home, a small church dating back to the 11th century lovely well-maintained gardens and extensive grounds. During the year this house served as one of the retreat centres for the school.

I was explaining my situation to a group of the London students when one of the group asked where will you live while at Oxford. I said that I had no idea as yet. He said why don't you live here at Waterperry House? It turned out this person was the Bursar of the estate and so I readily accepted and the 2nd door was opened.

Now I cannot attribute these coincidences to silence. All I can say is that when one does take time to quietly reflect and come into the still, silent present moment, then there is better chance that the decision made will be more attuned to the time and circumstances.

The year at Oxford was truly a sabbatical. It was in a way like a retreat. Certainly it was calmer compared to the days of running a business operating in 10 European countries. There was more time and space in a day to quietly consider different aspects of life and the options offered now with England as my new home. The old patterns were temporarily put aside as I enjoyed quiet walks around the *City of Dreaming Spires*, having conversations not designed to convince someone that they should buy something from you, and of course the opportunity to continue my education.

In addition to studying the history and principles of education, which was fascinating, there was also the opportunity to engage with my fellow students on the question of the use of technology in education. I arranged to provide them demonstrations of the most up-to-date education related hardware and software and then we discussed how it might be used and what impact it might have on students and teachers. The overall atmosphere of intellectual enquiry present in Oxford had its effect in that I found myself quite open to see what the result would be, as opposed to trying to sell an idea.

When it came time for me to prepare my final dissertation on the subject, I carefully reflected on what would be the approach that I would recommend. I spent a good deal of time sitting alone in a beautiful garden and eventually came to a conclusion. Although most of my fellow students were all for the extensive use of computers in the primary schools, I now did not believe that it would be suitable. I was sure that the expanding use of technology would eventually bring more computers into the classroom, but I had also seen the vital importance of the direct teacher/ student interface, especially for primary school children. Once again quiet reflection helped me see an issue more clearly and to make an important decision, one which I have continued to be satisfied with over the years.

After the course I began a new career in London as a self-employed consultant. Life continued in London and what followed was marriage to Judica and the subsequent arrival of two darling daughters, Jessica and Olivia, the founding and growth of a computer based training company and continued participation in a range of activities in the school and in the community.

A few years ago the school initiated a yearly silent retreat at one of their country estates. I soon became a regular attendee. For the last few years it has become a week- long event which has become one of the highlights of my year.

I have found this extensive period of silence in the presence of good company unique in terms of the depth of the peace and contentment experienced. On some of the walks around the grounds it became very clear that the substance of all I was observing; the trees, birds, sky and clouds are all of the same substance as myself. I found in fact that when the mind became still it no longer put a name on the form e.g. tree. Without that name what was seen was not differentiated from anything else, not even myself. The unity of the creation is truly experienced.

I have also found that study during such a periods of extended silence becomes very light and effortless. The meaning of even the most subtle scriptures seems to simply be revealed without the need for the moving mind to become engaged.

In conclusion, I would heartily recommend that you seek out the opportunity to spend an extended period of silence, ideally in the company of like-minded people. Once you have tasted the fruits of silence, the inner peace and contentment, the unity with all and everything, you will have a very clear reference point that will help guide your fine power of discrimination to make the right decisions in life.

Summary

As can be seen in this brief offering on the subject of silence, there is a great deal written on the subject. It might seem like a paradox that so many words are offered in an attempt to describe that which is without words, that which in fact is the source of words.

The main reason that this person put pen to paper, and then fingers to keyboard, is the general disdain that our current society seems to have for silence. Even some people whom I consider spiritually aware and virtuous, do not seem to accept that silence is one of the main keys to unlock our full inner spiritual power.

For others there seems to be a lack of understanding of the value of resting quietly in the present moment, with the body still and the mind quiet, not thinking about the past or conjecturing about the future.

The situation we are faced with comes down to a question of our values. Sound and activity are more valued in our society today, to such an extent that the natural states of silence and stillness are almost totally ignored, covered over, even knowingly avoided. In this unmeasured state, our physical, mental, and emotional energies are continually directed towards mechanical sounds and actions, which through repetition have become habitual.

We energetically shop in the market, trying sounds like this, activities like that, adding a little bit more of this type of sound and a bit more of that type of activity, giving little or no time for rest in silence and stillness. Is this your experience? If so, hopefully some of these words might inspire you to look afresh and avail yourself of the profound experience of true silence.

While this offering has focused on silence, it also quite naturally embraced stillness as well. They come together most clearly when we speak of the mind. A still mind is a quiet mind. There is no movement of thoughts, which is the same state as having no sounds in the mind. When there is true silence of the mind, when the thoughts have been quieted, then we experience real peace;

a state of true contentment, a state free from desires. In such a state we simply exist in the present moment. There is great rest, space and most importantly true and natural happiness. This happiness is not dependent on any external experience or any internal thought or feeling.

It just is.

This precious present is not something that someone gives you. It is a gift that you give yourself.

AND THE REST IS SILENCE

In Praise of Silence Bibliography

1001 Ways to Wisdom; Arcturus Publishing

Abba's Child: The Cry of the Heart for Intimate Belonging by Brennan Manning, NavPress

Anam Cara-Spiritual Wisdom for the Celtic World by John O Donohue; Bantam Books

And the Land Lay Still by James Robertson, Hamish Hamilton Bing Oneself, by F W Whiting; London School of Meditation

A Pocket Book on Virtue by Dadi Janki, Brahma Kumaris

Commentaries on Living by Krishnamurti, Quest Books

Counsels on the Spiritual Life by Thomas a' Kempis; Penguin Books

Good Company; The Study Society, London

I am That by Sri Nisargadatta Maharj, Chetana Ltd **Impressions of Theophrastus Such** by George Eliot, BiblioLife **Into a Silent Land** by Martin Laird; Darton, Longman & Todd

Journey to the Heart, Christian Contemplation Through the Centuries, Edited by Kim Nataraja; Canterbury Press

Justine by Lawrence Durrell, Penguin Books

Language & Silence: Essays on Language, Literature & the Inhuman by George Steiner, Yale University Press

Meditations-on the Monk Who Dwells in Daily Life by Thomas Moore; Harper Collins

Meditation: Man-Perfection in God-Satisfaction by Sri Chinmoy, Aum Publications

No Man Is an Island by Thomas Merton, Shambhala

Om Chanting and Meditation by Amit Ray, Inner Light Publishers

Presence - Working from Within. The Psychology of Being by Swami Dhyan Giten, Lulu.com

Reflections; London School of Meditation

Seeking Silence by Anthony Strano; Sterling Ethos

Silence as Yoga by Swami Paramananda, Sri Ramakrishna Math

Stillness Speaks by Eckhart Tolle; Hodder & Stoughton

The Classics of Western Spirituality- Conferences by John Cassian, Paulist Press **The Heart of Creation** by John Main, Edited by Laurence Freeman; Canterbury Press **The Little Prince** by Antoine de Saint-Exupéry, Harcourt, Inc

The Means and Manner of Obtaining Virtue by Benjamin Franklin; Penguin Books

The Modern Spirituality Series - John Main; Templegate Publishers

The Monk Who Sold His Ferrari by Robin S Shaw, Jaico Publishing House

The Notebook by Nicholas Sparks, Grand Central Publishing

The Power of Now: A Guide to Spiritual Enlightenment by Eckhart Tolle, New World Library

The Power of Silence by Father Richard Rohr; Bloomsbury Publishing

The Power of Silence by Graham Turner; Bloomsbury Publishing

The Prophet by Kahlil Gibran, Rupa & Co

The Selfless Self by Fr Laurence Freeman, Canterbury Press

The Sound of Silence (How to Find Inspiration in the Age of Information) by Michael Smith; Caux Books

The Spirit of Silence by John Lane; Green Books

The Supreme Yoga translated by Swami Venkatesananda, The Chiltern Yoga Trust

The Wisdom of Yoga: A Seeker's Guide to Extraordinary Living by Stephen Cope, Bantam

The Yoga Sutras by Swami Satchidananda, Integral Yoga Publications

Thoughts on Solitude by Thomas Merton; Shambala Publications

A cknowledgement and Thanks to the photographers and to the calligraphers and artists whose work has been photographed:

Jerome Toole

Paul Palmarozza

Alan Young

Trevor Waldron

Frederick Marnes

Charles Hardaker

AGuyTakingPhotos-CC

Websites:www.brainyquote.com; www.goodreads.com; www. mainquotes.com; www.searchquotes.com; www.values.com/ en.wikipedia.org;

Lightning Source UK Ltd.
Milton Keynes UK
UKIC01n2327041214
242684UK00009B/44